MAKING LIFE
A PRAYER

Selected Writings of **JOHN CASSIAN**

Upper Room Spiritual Classics — Series 1

Selected, edited, and introduced by
Keith Beasley-Topliffe

UPPER
ROOM BOOKS
NASHVILLE

Making Life a Prayer: Selected Writings of John Cassian
© 1997 by Upper Room Books. All Rights Reserved.

Art direction: Michele Wetherbee
Interior design and layout: Nancy Cole

First Printing: October 1997 (5)

Library of Congress Cataloging-in-Publication Data

Cassian, John, ca. 360–ca. 435.
   [Selections. English 1997]
   Making life a prayer : selected writings of John Cassian.
    p. cm. — (Upper Room spiritual classics. Series 1)
   ISBN 0-8358-0831-9 (pbk.)
   1. Monastic and religious life — Early works to 1800. 2. Spiritual life — Christianity — Early works to 1800. I. Title. II. Series.
BR65.C32E5 1997
248.4'814 — dc21   97-10158
                                    CIP

Printed in the United States of America

TABLE OF CONTENTS

INTRODUCTION

Christians are called to high ideals. Love God with all your being. Love your neighbor. Love your enemy. Pray without ceasing. It is hard to live these out in daily life. Maybe if we did not have so many distractions, so many responsibilities, we would have a chance.

In the fourth century, many Christians tried to escape the cares of city life to try to live a life of prayer in purity of heart in the deserts of Egypt and Syria. Some lived alone, others in communities. But they found that they faced many of the same problems: concern about food or possessions, temptations to pride or despair or vanity. Gradually they developed ways of dealing with these problems, a "wisdom of the desert."

John Cassian lived for many years among the monks and hermits of the desert, absorbing their wisdom. Then he summarized it and arranged it for the benefit of Christians attempting to live in community in western Europe. In this way he became a living bridge between the mothers and fathers of the desert and the nuns and monks of medieval Christendom.

The problems he addresses are still very much with us, though. His vision of the goals of the Christian life and his advice on how to avoid roadblocks on the way still speak to us. His advice on prayer has been "rediscovered" in recent writings on what is sometimes called breath prayer.

CASSIAN'S WORLD

By the beginning of the fourth century, the Roman Empire was clearly in decline. Barbarian armies were pushing back the borders and making raids deep into the heartland. After nearly three centuries of persecution, Christianity was legalized in 313 and soon became the official religion of the empire. Some Christians viewed this as a mixed blessing. If becoming Christian was the politically correct thing to do, then people might become Christian in appearance only. How could people maintain the pure ideals of Christian life under such circumstances?

Even before Emperor Constantine officially tolerated Christianity, an Egyptian named Antony had moved to a mountain cave in the desert between the Nile and the Red Sea. There he lived in solitude, sometimes not emerging from the cave for months. Eventually others, men and women, came to seek his wisdom on "spiritual combat." Some of them found their own solitary places in the desert. They were called "eremites" (or hermits) from the Greek word for "desert." Others built communities in the salt marshes of the Nile Delta, along the upper Nile, in the Holy Land, or in the Syrian desert. They were called "cenobites" from the Greek for "common life." The community buildings were called monasteries. Some who became noted for their own wisdom were given the title Abba or Amma (Aramaic words that mean Papa or Mama). Leaders of communities were called Presbyters (Elders).

When Bishop Athanasius of Alexandria wrote a

biography of Antony shortly after Antony's death in 356, his example gained even wider influence. The original Greek was read throughout the eastern empire, and a Latin translation spread it to the West. Some, like Augustine whose conversion was sparked by reading it in 386, founded small communities of their own with varying degrees of success.

CASSIAN'S LIFE

John Cassian was born sometime before (or during) 365. Where is not certain. Perhaps it was Gaul (today, southern France), where he returned in later years. Perhaps it was in what today is Romania, since one ancient author calls him a Scythian. He was apparently well educated and left home as a teenager. With his friend Germanus, he joined a monastery in Bethlehem near the cave reputed to be the birthplace of Jesus. After a few years there, he and Germanus left for Egypt. They were supposed to visit some of the communities and hermits, learn what they could, and bring a report back to Bethlehem. They stayed in Egypt for seven years. After a brief return to Bethlehem, they went back to Egypt for more visiting.

About 400 they left for Constantinople (Istanbul, today), the capital of the eastern empire. They joined the staff of John Chrysostom, the patriarch, who ordained Cassian a deacon. When Chrysostom became embroiled in controversy in 404, he sent Cassian and Germanus to seek help from Pope Innocent I. Innocent ordained Cassian to the priesthood. After several years in Rome, Cassian moved to Marseilles. There he founded two monasteries, one for men and one for women.

Around 420, he wrote his first book, *The Institutes of the Communities* (or *Cenobia*). A few years later he wrote a summary of the teachings of the desert fathers, presented as a series of spiritual conferences with fifteen famous abbas of the desert. These *Conferences* were followed by a doctrinal work, *On the Incarnation of Christ Against Nestorius*, in which he quotes extensively from Scripture and from his teachers and contemporaries, including Chrysostom, Augustine, Jerome, and Ambrose. He argues for the full divinity of Christ incarnate as fully human in one divine-human person. Nestorius had argued for a dual personality, one divine, one human. This work was published in 430. Cassian died after 432, perhaps about 435.

More than a century later, Benedict of Nursia, in drawing up a rule for monastic life, borrowed heavily from *Institutes*. He also recommended that *Institutes* and *Conferences* be read regularly for the dinnertime education of monks. Thanks in part to this recommendation, Cassian has continued to have an influence on Christian spirituality.

FURTHER READING

The works of John Cassian have not been completely translated into English. The most complete edition is the 1894 translation of E. C. S. Gibson, found in *Nicene and Post-Nicene Fathers*, Series II, volume XI. Large portions were omitted due to the translator's Victorian sensitivities. A recent translation by Colm Luibheid of nine of the twenty-four *Conferences* is available from Paulist Press. The standard English study of Cassian's life and work is *John Cassian* by Owen Chadwick.

The *Life of Antony* by Athanasius has been published in English by Paulist Press. *The Sayings of the Desert Fathers* (including some of the Desert Mothers), *The Lives of the Desert Fathers*, and *Harlots of the Desert* (four stories of penitent women who sought new lives in the desert) are all available from Cistercian Publications. *The Wisdom of the Desert*, selected, translated, and introduced by Thomas Merton, is a New Directions Book. *The Rule of Saint Benedict* is available in various editions. An excellent introduction to its use today by "ordinary" Christians is *Wisdom Distilled from the Daily* by Joan Chittister, O.S.B., from HarperSanFrancisco.

NOTE ON THE TEXT

These selections are based on Gibson's translation. They have been abridged and the language and punctuation modernized. They have been edited for inclusive language. Scripture quotations and allusions have been italicized and conformed where possible to the New Revised Standard Version.

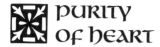 # PURITY
OF HEART

John Cassian wrote Conferences *for the monks in the community he founded in Provence about 428. Through a series of spiritual conversations with various of the desert fathers, he presents the essentials of Egyptian spirituality and community living. In this first conference, Abba Moses talks about the goal of being a monk.*

Whenever those whose business it is to use weapons of war want to show their skill, they try to shoot their arrows or darts into certain small targets that have the prizes painted on them. They know that they cannot in any other way than by the line of their aim secure the prize they hope for. But if the target happens to be withdrawn from their sight, they cannot perceive that they have strayed from the direction of the intended straight line because they have no mark to prove the skillfulness of their aim. So then the end indeed that we have set before us is, as the apostle says, eternal life, as he declares, *"The advantage you get is sanctification. The end is eternal life."* But the immediate goal is purity of heart, which he not unfairly terms "sanctification," without which this end cannot be gained. Of this goal the same blessed apostle teaches us and significantly uses the very term, saying, *"Forgetting what lies behind and straining forward to what lies ahead, I press on toward the goal for the prize of the heavenly call of God in Christ Jesus."* Whatever then can help to guide us to this object, that is, purity of heart, we must follow with all our might. But whatever hinders us from it, we must shun as a dangerous and hurtful thing. For this we do and endure all things. For this we make light of our kinfolk, our country, honors, riches, the delights of this world, and all kinds of pleasures. And so when this object is set before us, we shall always direct our actions and thoughts straight toward the attainment of it. If it is not constantly fixed before our eyes, it will not only make all our toils vain and useless, but it will also excite all kinds of thoughts opposed to one another. For the mind is sure to rove about from hour to hour and minute to minute in all sorts of wandering thoughts.

In the case of some who have despised the greatest possessions of this world, and not only large sums of gold and silver but also large properties, we have seen them afterwards disturbed and excited over a knife or pencil or pin or pen. If they kept their gaze steadily fixed out of a pure heart, they would certainly never allow such a thing to happen for trifles. When they have given up all their wealth for the love of Christ, yet preserve their former disposition in the matter of trifles and are sometimes quickly upset about them, they become in all points barren and unfruitful. They are without the love of which the apostle speaks: *"If I give away all my possessions, and if I hand over my body so that I may boast, but do not have love, I gain nothing."* And from this it clearly follows that perfection is not arrived at simply by self-denial, the giving up of all our goods, and the casting away of honors unless there is that love, the details of which the apostle describes. That love consists in purity of heart alone. For not to be *envious or boastful or arrogant or rude,* not to *insist on* one's *own way,* not to *rejoice in wrongdoing,* not to think evil, and so on—what is all this except always to offer to God a perfect and clean heart and to keep it free from all disturbances?

Everything should be done and sought after by us for the sake of this. For this we must seek solitude. For this we submit to fasting, vigils, toils, bodily nakedness, reading, and all other virtues that through them we may be enabled to prepare our hearts and to keep them unharmed by all evil passions, and resting on these steps to mount to the perfection of love. Those things that are of secondary importance, we ought to practice with a view to our main object, that is, purity of heart, which is love. As long as it is still found in us intact and unharmed, we shall not be hurt if any of the things that are of secondary importance are necessarily omitted. Therefore fasting, vigils, meditation on the Scriptures, self-denial, and giving up all possessions are not perfection but aids to perfection. The end of that science does not lie in these, but by means of these we arrive at the end. Whatever can disturb that purity and peace of mind—even though it may seem useful and valuable—should be shunned as really hurtful. By this rule we shall succeed in escaping harm from mistakes and vagaries and make straight for the desired end and reach it.

This then should be our main effort, and this steadfast purpose of heart we should constantly aspire after: that the soul may always cling to God and to heavenly things. We have an excellent illustration of this state of mind and condition in the Gospel in the case of Martha and Mary. Martha was performing a service that was certainly a sacred one, since she was ministering to the Lord and his disciples. Mary, being intent only on spiritual instruction, was clinging close to the feet of Jesus, which she kissed and anointed with the ointment of a good confession. Martha, toiling with pious care, asks for the help of her sister from the Lord, saying, *"Lord, do you not care that my sister has left me to do all the work by myself? Tell her then to help me."* Certainly it was to no unworthy work but to a praiseworthy service that she summoned her. But what does she hear from the Lord? *"Martha, Martha, you are worried and distracted by many things; there is need of only one thing."* You see then that the Lord makes the chief good consist in meditation, in divine contemplation. From this we see that all other virtues should be put in the second place, even though we admit that they are necessary, useful, and excellent, because they are all performed for the sake of this one thing. For when the Lord says, *"You are worried and distracted by many things; there is need of only one thing,"* he makes the primary good consist not in practical work, however praiseworthy and rich in fruits it may be, but in contemplation of him, which indeed is simple and *"only one."* Therefore *"Mary has chosen the better part, which will not be taken away from her."* Although he says nothing of Martha and certainly does not appear to blame her, yet in praising the one he implies that the other is inferior. Again when he says *"which will not be taken away from her,"* he shows that from the other her portion can be taken away. For a bodily ministry cannot last forever, but this one's desire can never have an end.

☩ tHE SpIRItUAL AtHLEtE

From *Institutes of the Communities*, Book 5,
Chapters 17–21

Cassian's Institutes *was written earlier than* Conferences *and begins with practical rules for monastic living—what to wear, how much to eat, when to pray, and which psalms to use in praying. The later parts are concerned with the eight "principal faults" that can hinder spiritual progress. This portrait of the spiritual athlete is taken from the discussion of gluttony.*

Would you like to hear a true athlete of Christ striving according to the rules and laws of the conflict? *"I,"* said he, *"do not run aimlessly, nor do I box as though beating the air; but I punish my body and enslave it, so that after proclaiming to others I myself should not be disqualified."* You see how he made the chief part of the struggle depend upon himself, that is upon his flesh, as if on a most sure foundation, and placed the result of the battle simply in the chastisement of the flesh and the subjection of his body. *"I do not run aimlessly,"* he says. He does not run aimlessly because, looking to the heavenly Jerusalem, he has a mark set, toward which his heart is swiftly directed without swerving. He does not run aimlessly, because, he says, *"forgetting what lies behind and straining forward to what lies ahead, I press on toward the goal for the prize of the heavenly call of God in Christ Jesus"* toward which he ever directs his mental gaze, and hastening toward it with all speed of heart, proclaims with confidence, *"I have fought the good fight, I have finished the race, I have kept the faith."* And because he knows he has run untiringly, he boldly concludes, *"From now on there is reserved for me the crown of righteousness, which the Lord, the righteous judge, will give me on that day."* And that he might open up to us also a similar hope of reward, he adds, *"and not only to me but also to all who have longed for his appearing."* We shall be sharers of his crown in the day of judgment if we love the coming of Christ.

He also testifies that he has conquered in another kind of contest, saying, *"Nor do I box as though beating the air; but I punish my body and enslave it."* And this properly has to do with the pains of abstinence, bodily fasting, and affliction of the flesh. He means by this that he is a vigorous bruiser of his own flesh, and he points out that not in vain has he planted his blows of self-control against it. He has gained a battle triumph by mortifying his own body; for when it is chastised with the blows of self-control and struck down with the boxing gloves of fasting, he has secured for his victorious spirit the crown of immortality and the prize of incorruption.

Athletes of Christ, as long as they are in the body, never lack a victory to be gained in contests. In the proportion that they grow by triumphant successes so does a severer kind of struggle confront them. When the flesh is subdued and conquered, what swarms of foes, what hosts of enemies are incited by their triumphs and rise up against the victorious soldiers of Christ! So if we want to rise with ever-growing virtue to these stages of triumph, we ought to enter the battle and begin by saying with the apostle, *"Nor do I box as though beating the air; but I punish my body and enslave it."* When this conflict is ended we may be able to say with him, *"Our struggle is not against enemies of blood and flesh, but against the rulers, against the authorities, against the cosmic powers of this present darkness, against the spiritual forces of evil in the heavenly places."* We cannot possibly join battle with them nor deserve to make trial of spiritual combats if we are baffled in a battle with the belly.

Self-indulgence must be cut off in the same way that the sin of unchastity has to be rooted out. For if you are unable to check the unnecessary desires of the appetite, how will you be able to extinguish the fire of lust? And if you are not able to control passions that are openly manifest and small, how will you be able to fight against those that are secret and excite you, when none are there to see? So strength of mind is tested in separate impulses and in any sort of passion. If it is overcome in the case of very small and obvious desires, how will it endure in those that are really great and powerful and hidden?

It is not an external enemy we dread. Our foe is shut up within ourselves. An internal warfare is daily waged by us. If we are victorious in this, all external things will be made weak, and everything will be made peaceful and subdued for the soldier of Christ. Let us not believe that an external fast from visible food alone can possibly be sufficient for perfection of heart and purity of body unless with it there has also been united a fast of the soul. For the soul also has its foods that are harmful. Slander is its food, and indeed one that is very dear to it. A burst of anger also supplies it with miserable food for an hour and destroys it as well with its deadly savor. Envy is a food of the mind, corrupting it with its poisonous juices and never ceasing to make it wretched and miserable at the prosperity and success of another. Vanity is its food, which gratifies the mind with a delicious meal for a time but afterwards strips it clear and bare of all virtue. Then vanity dismisses it barren and void of all spiritual fruit. All lust and shifty wanderings of heart are a sort of food for the soul, nourishing it on harmful meats, but leaving it afterwards without a share of the heavenly bread and of really solid food. If then, with all the powers we have, we abstain from these in a most holy fast, our observance of the bodily fast will be both useful and profitable. For labor of the flesh, when joined with contrition of the spirit, will produce a sacrifice that is most acceptable to God and a worthy shrine of holiness in the pure and undefiled inmost chambers of the heart. But if, while fasting as far as the body is concerned, we are entangled in the most dangerous vices of the soul, our humiliation of the flesh will do us no good whatever.

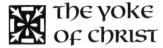 # the yoke
# of christ

From *Conferences*, Conference 24, Chapters 22–24

This final conference is with Abba Abraham. It begins with
a question from Germanus, Cassian's companion during his
travels in the deserts of Syria and Egypt.

GERMANUS: We beg you to explain to us something that is said in the Gospel: *"My yoke is easy, and*
my burden is light." For the apostle says, *"Indeed, all*
who want to live a godly life in Christ Jesus will be
persecuted." But whatever is hard and filled with persecutions cannot be easy and light.

ABRAHAM: We can prove by the easy teaching
of our own experience that our Lord and Savior's
saying is perfectly true if we approach the way of
perfection properly and in accordance with Christ's
will. If we mortify all our desires, cut off harmful
pleasures, and not only allow nothing to remain with
us of this world's goods but actually recognize that
we are not our own masters, then we truly make our
own the apostle's words: *"It is no longer I who live, but*
it is Christ who lives in me." For what can be burden-
some or hard to those who have embraced with their
whole hearts the yoke of Christ? They are estab-
lished in true humility and ever fix their eyes on the
Lord's sufferings and rejoice in all the wrongs that
are offered them, saying, *"Therefore I am content with*
weaknesses, insults, hardships, persecutions, and calamities

for the sake of Christ; for whenever I am weak, then I am strong." By what loss of any common thing, I ask, will they be injured, who boast of perfect renunciation, and voluntarily reject for Christ's sake all the pomp of this world, and consider all and every of its desires as dung, so that they may gain Christ? By continual meditation on this command of the gospel, they scorn and get rid of agitation at every loss: *For what will it profit them if they gain the whole world but forfeit their life? Or what will they give in return for their life?* What loss will vex those who recognize that everything that can be taken away from others is not their own? They proclaim with unconquered valor: *"We brought nothing into the world, so that we can take nothing out of it."* What want will overcome their courage? Like the apostle, they glory *"in toil and hardship, through many a sleepless night, hungry and thirsty, often without food, cold and naked."* What effort or what hard command of an elder can disturb their peace, who have no will of their own, and not only patiently but even gratefully accept what is commanded? After the example of our Savior, they do not seek their own will but the Father's, as Christ says himself to his Father, *"Yet not what I want but what you want."* By what wrongs also, by what persecution will they be frightened? What punishment can fail to be delightful to those who always rejoice (together with apostles) in stripes and long to be counted worthy to suffer shame for the name of Christ?

But the fact that to us on the contrary the yoke of Christ seems neither light nor easy must be rightly ascribed to our perverseness. We are cast down by unbelief and lack of faith. We fight with foolish stubbornness against Christ's command, or rather advice: *"If you wish to be perfect, go, sell your possessions; . . . then come, follow me."* We keep the substance of our worldly goods. The devil holds our souls fast in the toils of these. When he wants to cut us off from spiritual delights, he irritates us by diminishing these goods and depriving us of them. When the sweetness of Christ's yoke and lightness of his burden have become grievous to us through the evil of a corrupt desire and we are caught in the chains of property and substance that we kept for our comfort and solace, the devil can always torment us with the scourges of worldly cares. For *"they are caught in the toils of their sin,"* and hear from the prophet: *"All of you are kindlers of fire, lighters of firebrands. Walk in the flame of your fire, and among the brands that you have kindled!"* As Solomon is witness, *"One is punished by the very things by which one sins."* The very pleasures we enjoy become a torment to us, and the delights and enjoyments of this flesh turn on us like executioners. Those who are supported by their wealth and property are sure not to admit perfect humility into their hearts nor put to death all dangerous pleasures. But where these tools of goodness give their aid, all the trials of this present life and whatever losses the enemy can contrive are endured not only with the utmost patience, but with real pleasure. But when they are lacking, so dangerous a pride springs up that we are actually wounded by the deadly strokes of impatience at the slightest reproach. How then is it that the wondrous sweetness of the Lord's yoke is felt to be bitter, but because the bitterness of our dislike injures it? How is it that the exceeding lightness of the divine burden becomes heavy, but because in our obstinate presumption we despise him by whom it was borne? But all who truly give up this world and take upon themselves Christ's yoke and learn of him and are trained in the daily practice of suffering wrong will always remain undisturbed by all temptations.

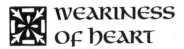

WEARINESS
OF HEART

From *Institutes of the Communities*, Book 10,
Chapters 1–6

*Weariness of heart (a step beyond simple boredom) is
another of the impediments to spiritual growth Cassian
discusses. He says it comes particularly in the middle of the
day, the "sixth hour." He presents a portrait of a monk
afflicted with this spirit.*

Our sixth combat is with what we may term
weariness or distress of heart. This is akin to dejection and is a dangerous and frequent foe to dwellers
in the desert. It is especially disturbing to a monk
about the sixth hour, like some fever that seizes him
at stated times, bringing the burning heat of its
attacks on the sick man at usual and regular hours.

And when this has taken possession of some
unhappy soul, it produces dislike of the place, disgust
with the cell, and disdain and contempt of the
brethren who dwell with him or at a little distance, as
if they were careless or unspiritual. It also makes the
man lazy and sluggish about all manner of work that
has to be done within the enclosure of his dormitory.
It does not let him stay in his cell or take any pains
about reading. He often groans because he can do no
good while he stays there, and he complains and
sighs because he can bear no spiritual fruit so long as
he is joined to that society. He complains that he is
cut off from spiritual gain and is of no use in the

place. He acts as if he could lead others and be useful to a great number of people, yet he is not profiting anyone by his teaching and doctrine. He daydreams of distant monasteries and describes such places as more profitable and better suited for salvation. He paints the life there as sweet and full of spirituality. On the other hand, he says that everything about him is rough. Not only is there nothing edifying among the others there, but even food for the body cannot be procured without great difficulty. Finally, he fancies that he will never be well while he stays in that place unless he leaves his cell and takes off from there as quickly as possible. Then the fifth or sixth hour brings him such bodily weariness and longing for food that he seems to himself worn out as if with a long journey or some very heavy work or as if he had put off taking food during a fast of two or three days. He looks about anxiously this way and that and sighs that none come to see him. He often goes in and out of his cell and frequently gazes up at the sun, as if it were too slow in setting. So a kind of unreasonable confusion of mind takes possession of him like some foul darkness and makes him idle and useless for every spiritual work. He imagines that no cure for so terrible an attack can be found in anything except visiting someone or in the comfort of sleep. Then the disease suggests that he ought to show courteous and friendly hospitalities to the brothers and pay visits to the sick, whether near at hand or far off. He talks too about some dutiful and religious offices. Those kinfolk ought to be inquired after. He ought to go and see them oftener. It would be a real work of piety to go more frequently to visit that religious woman, devoted to the service of God, who is deprived of all support of kindred. It would be a most excellent thing to get what is needful for her who is neglected and despised by her own kinfolk. He ought piously to devote his time to these things instead of staying uselessly and with no profit in his cell.

And so the wretched soul, embarrassed by such contrivances of the enemy, is disturbed until, worn out by weariness of heart as by some strong battering ram, it sinks into slumber. Or, driven out from the confinement of its cell, it seeks consolation under these attacks in visiting some brother, only to be afterwards weakened the more by this remedy. For the enemy will more frequently and more severely attack one who looks for safety neither in victory nor in fighting but in flight. Little by little he is drawn away from his cell and begins to forget the object of his profession, that is nothing but meditation and contemplation of that divine purity that excels all things and that can only be gained by silence and prayer.

True Christian athletes who desire to strive for perfection should hasten to expel this disease also from the recesses of their souls and strive against this most evil spirit of weariness of heart in both directions, so that they may neither fall stricken through by the shaft of slumber nor be driven out from the community, even though under some pious excuse or pretext, and depart as runaways.

# SPIRITUAL DRYNESS

From *Conferences*, Conference 4, Chapters 2–5

The conference with Abba Daniel is mostly about the struggle between the desires of flesh and spirit. But it begins with this discussion of the causes of spiritual dryness in prayer.

We asked this blessed Daniel why it was that as we sat in the cells we were sometimes filled with the utmost gladness of heart, together with inexpressible delight and an abundance of the holiest feelings. Pure prayers were readily breathed, and the mind, being filled with spiritual fruits and praying to God even in sleep, could feel that its petitions rose lightly and powerfully to God. Then for no reason we were suddenly filled with the utmost grief and were weighed down with unreasonable depression. We not only felt as if we ourselves were overcome with such feelings, but also our cell grew dreadful, reading bored us, and our prayers were offered up unsteadily and vaguely, almost as if we were intoxicated. While we were groaning and endeavoring to restore ourselves to our former disposition, the mind was unable to do this. The more earnestly it sought to fix again its gaze upon God, the more strongly it was carried away to wandering thoughts and so utterly deprived of all spiritual fruits that it could not be roused from this deadly slumber even by the desire of the kingdom of heaven or by the fear of hell. This is how he replied.

A threefold account of this mental dryness of which you speak has been given by the elders. For it comes either from carelessness on our part, or from the assaults of the devil, or from the permission and allowance of the Lord. From carelessness on our part, when through our own faults, coldness has come upon us, and we have behaved carelessly and hastily. Owing to slothful idleness we have fed on bad thoughts, and so the ground of the heart brings forth thorns and thistles. They spring up in it and make us sterile and powerless in all spiritual fruit and meditation. From the assaults of the devil when, sometimes, while we are actually intent on good desires, our enemy with crafty subtlety makes his way into the heart. Without our knowledge and against our will we are drawn away from the best intentions.

But for God's permission and allowance there is a twofold reason. First, being for a short time forsaken by the Lord and observing with all humility the weakness of our own heart, we may not be puffed up on account of the previous purity of heart granted to us by God's visitation. By showing that when we are forsaken by God we cannot possibly recover our former state of purity and delight by any groaning and efforts of our own, we may also learn that our previous gladness of heart resulted not from our own earnestness but from God's gift. For the present time, it must be sought once more from his grace and enlightenment. But a second reason for this allowance is to test our perseverance and steadfastness of mind and real desires. It shows in us with what purpose of heart or earnest prayer we seek the return of the Holy Spirit. We discover with what efforts we must seek that spiritual gladness—when once it is lost—and the joy of purity. We learn to preserve it more carefully, when once it is secured, and to hold it with firmer grasp. For people are generally more careless about keeping whatever they think can be easily replaced.

By this it is clearly shown that God's grace and mercy always work in us what is good, and that when they forsake us, the worker's efforts are useless. However earnestly we may strive, we cannot regain our former condition without God's help. This saying is constantly fulfilled in our case: *"It depends not on human will or exertion, but on God who shows mercy."* On the other hand, this grace sometimes does not refuse to visit even the careless and indifferent with that holy inspiration of which you spoke. It does so with an abundance of spiritual thoughts. It inspires the unworthy, arouses the sleepers, and enlightens those who are blinded by ignorance. It mercifully reproves us and chastens us, shedding itself abroad in our hearts so that we may be stirred by the sorrow that God excites and driven to rise from the sleep of sloth.

 CONVICTION

From *Conferences*, Conference 9, Chapters 26–30

The heart of Conferences *is the pair of conversations with Abba Isaac on prayer. Here he talks about a key theme in desert spirituality: the holy conviction that can be either assurance of God's mercy or sorrow (compunction) for sin.*

But who is able, with whatever experience he may be endowed, to give a sufficient account of the varieties and reasons and grounds of conviction by which the mind is inflamed and set on fire and incited to pure and most fervent prayers? Sometimes a verse of any one of the Psalms gives us an occasion of ardent prayer while we are singing. A spiritual conference has often raised the affections of those present to the richest prayer. We are no less carried away to full conviction by the death of someone dear to us. The recollection of our coldness and carelessness has sometimes aroused in us a healthful fervor of spirit. No one can doubt that numberless opportunities are not lacking, by which through God's grace the coldness and sleepiness of our minds can be shaken off.

It is no less difficult to trace out how convictions are produced from the inmost recesses of the soul. Often through some inexpressible delight and keenness of spirit the fruit of conviction arises so that it actually breaks forth into shouts owing to the greatness of its uncontrollable joy. The delight of the heart and greatness of exultation make themselves heard. But sometimes the mind hides itself in complete silence within the secrets of a profound quiet so that the amazement of a sudden illumination chokes all sounds of words, and the overawed spirit either keeps all its feelings to itself or loses them and pours forth its desires to God with *sighs too deep for words*. And sometimes it is filled with such overwhelming conviction and grief that it cannot express it except by floods of tears.

GERMANUS: My own poor self is not altogether ignorant of this feeling of conviction. For often when tears arise at the memory of my faults, I have, by the Lord's visitation, been so refreshed by this ineffable joy you describe that the greatness of the joy has assured me that I ought not to despair of their forgiveness. There is nothing more sublime if only it could be recalled at our own will. For sometimes when I want to stir myself up with all my power to the same conviction and tears and place before my eyes all my faults and sins, I am unable to bring back those copious tears. My eyes are dry and hard like some hardest flint. Not a single tear trickles from them. As much as I congratulate myself for copious tears, just so I mourn that I cannot bring them back again whenever I wish.

ISAAC: Not every kind of shedding of tears is produced by one feeling or one virtue. One kind of weeping is caused by the pricks of our sins wounding our hearts, of which we read: *"I am weary with my moaning; every night I flood my bed with tears; I drench my couch with my weeping.*" And again: "*Let tears stream down like a torrent day and night! Give yourself no rest, your eyes no respite!*" Another arises from the contemplation of eternal good things and the desire of that future glory, so that even richer wellsprings of tears burst forth from uncontrollable delights and boundless exultation. The soul is athirst for the mighty Living God, saying, "*When shall I come and behold the face of God? My tears have been my food day and night.*" In another way the tears flow forth without any conscience of deadly sin, yet still proceeding from the fear of hell and the recollection of that terrible judgment. The psalmist was struck with this terror and prayed to God: "*Do not enter into judgment with your servant, for no one living is righteous before you.*" There is also another kind of tears, caused not by knowledge of oneself but by the hardness and sins of others. Samuel is described as having wept for Saul. Both the Lord in the Gospel and Jeremiah in former days wept for the city of Jerusalem. Jeremiah said, "*O that my head were a spring of water, and my eyes a fountain of tears, so that I might weep day and night for the slain of my poor people!*" There are also those tears of which we hear in Psalm 102: "*For I eat ashes like bread, and mingle tears with my drink.*" These were due to the anxieties of this life and its distresses and losses by which the righteous who are living in this world are oppressed. This is clearly shown not only by the words of the psalm itself, but also by its title, which runs as follows: "*A prayer of one afflicted, when faint and pleading before the Lord.*"

These tears are vastly different from those that are squeezed out from dry eyes while the heart is hard. We cannot believe that these are altogether fruitless, for the attempt to shed them is made with a good intention, especially by those who have not yet been able to attain to perfect knowledge or to be thoroughly cleansed from the stains of past or present sins. But certainly the flow of tears ought not to be forced out by those who have already advanced to the love of virtue. Even if it is produced, it will never attain the rich copiousness of spontaneous tears. For it will rather cast down the soul and draw it away from the celestial heights where the awed mind of one who prays should be steadfastly fixed.

GOD'S GRACE AND OUR ACTION

From *Institutes of the Communities*, Book 12,
Chapters 13–16

The final barrier to spiritual growth discussed in Institutes
*is pride (the others, in addition to gluttony and weariness of
heart mentioned earlier, are love of money, fornication,
anger, dejection, and vanity). In this selection, Cassian
returns to a subject discussed under each of these barriers:
how we are powerless to overcome the fault except by the
grace of God.*

The abbas in the desert have not painted the
way of perfection and its character in high-sounding
words. Rather, possessing it in deed and truth and in
the virtue of their spirit, they have passed it on by
their own experience and sure example. They say
that people cannot be completely cleansed from sins
of the flesh without realizing that all human labors
and efforts are insufficient for so great and perfect an
end. They must be taught, not by the system handed
down to them, but by their feelings and virtues and
their own experience, that it can only be gained by
the mercy and assistance of God. For in order to gain
such splendid and lofty prizes of purity and perfection, however great may be the efforts of fasting and
vigils and readings and solitude and retirement
applied to it, they will not be sufficient to secure it by
the merits of the actual efforts and toil. Human

exertions will never make up for the lack of the divine gift unless it is granted by divine compassion in answer to prayer.

I do not say this to belittle human efforts or in an attempt to discourage any from working and doing their best. But clearly and most earnestly I insist, not giving my own opinion but that of the elders, that perfection cannot possibly be gained without these efforts. But by these only and without the grace of God no one one can ever attain it. For when we say that human efforts cannot of themselves secure it without the aid of God, we thus insist that God's mercy and grace are bestowed only upon those who labor and exert themselves. For we say, in accordance with our Savior's words, that *"everyone who asks receives, and everyone who searches finds, and for everyone who knocks, the door will be opened."* But the asking, seeking, and knocking on our part are insufficient unless the mercy of God gives what we ask, opens where we knock, and enables us to find what we seek. God is at hand to give all these things, if only we give God the opportunity by our goodwill. God desires and looks for our perfection and salvation far more than we do ourselves. The blessed David knew so well that by his own efforts he could not secure the increase of his work and labor, that he entreated with renewed prayers: *"Prosper for us the work of our hands—O prosper the work of our hands!"*

And so, if we wish in very deed and truth to attain to the crown of virtues, we ought to listen to those teachers and guides who, not dreaming with pompous declamations but learning by act and experience, are able to teach us, direct us, and show us the road by which we may arrive at it. They testify that they have themselves reached it by faith rather than by any merits of their efforts. Further, the purity of heart that they have gained has taught them this above all: to recognize more and more that they are burdened with sin. Their compunction for their faults increases day by day as their purity of soul advances. They sigh continually from the bottom of their hearts because they see that they cannot possibly avoid the spots and blemishes of those faults that are ingrained in them through countless trifling thoughts. And therefore they declared that they looked for the reward of the future life, not from the merits of their works, but from the mercy of the Lord. They take no credit for their great circumspection of heart in comparison with others, since they ascribed this not to their own exertions but to divine grace. Without flattering themselves on account of the carelessness of those who are cold, instead they aimed at a lasting humility by fixing their gaze on those whom they knew to be really free from sin and already in the enjoyment of eternal bliss in the kingdom of heaven. By this consideration they avoided the downfall of pride, and at the same time always saw both what they were aiming at and what they had to grieve over. They knew that they could not attain that purity of heart for which they yearned while weighed down by the burden of the flesh.

So, according to their teaching and instruction,

we should press toward it and be diligent in fasting, vigils, prayers, and contrition of heart and body for fear lest all these things should be rendered useless by an attack of pride. For we ought to believe not merely that we cannot secure this actual perfection by our own efforts and exertions, but that we cannot even perform these things without the help of divine protection and the grace of God's inspiration, chastisement, and exhortation.

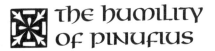# the humility of pinufius

From *Institutes of the Communities*, Book 4,
Chapters 30–31

In the fourth book of Institutes, *Cassian discusses the
character of a monk and, above all, the paired virtues of
obedience and humility. He concludes this discussion with
the example of the life of Abba Pinufius.*

Abba Pinufius, when he was elder of a huge community in the Nile Delta of northern Egypt, was held in
honor and respect by all out of reverence either for
his life or his age or his priesthood. When he saw
that for this reason he could not practice the humility
he longed for with all the ardor of his disposition and
had no opportunity of exercising the virtue of subjection that he desired, he fled secretly from the community and withdrew alone into the farthest parts of the
southern desert. There he laid aside the habit of the
monks and assumed secular dress. Thus dressed, he
sought the community that he knew to be the strictest
of all. He fancied that he would not be known there
owing to the distance of the spot, or else that he
could easily stay hidden there due to the size of the
monastery and the number of brothers. There he
remained for a long time at the entrance and as a
suppliant at the knees of the brothers he sought with
most earnest prayers to gain admission. He was at
last admitted with much scorn as a feeble old man

who had lived all his life in the world and had asked in his old age to be allowed to enter a community when he could no longer gratify his passions. As they said that he was seeking this not for the sake of religion but because he was compelled by hunger and want, they gave him the care and management of the garden as he seemed an old man and not specially fitted for any particular work. This he performed under another, younger brother who kept him by him as entrusted to him. He was so subordinate to him and cultivated the desired virtue of humility so obediently that he daily performed with the utmost diligence not only everything that had to do with the care and management of the garden but also all those duties that were looked on by the others as hard, degrading, and disagreeable. In addition, he rose by night to do many things secretly without anyone looking on or knowing it. Darkness concealed him so that no one could discover the author of the deed. When he had hidden himself there for three years and had been sought for high and low by the brothers all through Egypt, he was at last seen but could scarcely be recognized owing to the meanness of his dress and the humble character of the duty he was performing. For he was stooping down and hoeing the ground for vegetables and bringing dung on his shoulders and laying it about their roots. Seeing this, the brother hesitated for a long time in recognizing him. But at last he came nearer, and taking careful note not only of his looks but also of the tone of his voice, he immediately fell at his feet. At first, all who saw it were struck with the greatest astonishment why he should do this to one they regarded as the lowest of all, a novice who had but lately forsaken the world. Afterward, they were struck with still greater wonder when he announced his name, which was one that had been well known among them by repute. All the brothers asked his pardon for their former ignorance because they had for so long classed him with the juniors and children. They brought him back to his own community, against his will and in tears because by the envy of the devil he had been cheated out of a worthy mode of life and the humility that he had rejoiced to discover after his long search, and because he had not succeeded in ending his life in that state of subjection that he had secured. They guarded him with the utmost care in case he should slip away again in the same sort of way and escape from them also.

And when he had stayed there for a little while, he was again seized with a longing and desire for humility. Taking advantage of the silence of night, he made his escape in such a way that this time he sought no neighboring district but regions that were unknown and strange and separated by a wide distance. Embarking in a ship, he managed to travel to Palestine, believing that he would more securely lie hidden in those places where his name had never been heard. When he had arrived, he immediately sought out our own monastery that was at no great distance from the cave in which our Lord was born of a virgin. And though he concealed himself here for some time, yet like *a city built on a hill* (to use our Lord's expression) he could not long be hidden. Soon some brothers who had come to the holy places from Egypt to pray recognized him and recalled him with most fervent prayers to his own community.

✠ RENUNCIATION OF THE WORLD

From *Institutes of the Communities*, Book 4,
Chapters 32–36

*Cassian follows the story of Pinufius with a sermon he
preached to new monks being received into a community.
Such candidates would have to prove the sincerity of their
desire, as well as patience and humility, by lying outside the
entrance of the monastery until the monks chose to admit
them—ten days or more.*

You know that after lying for so many days at
the entrance you are today to be admitted. And to
begin with you ought to know the reason of the difficulty put in your way. For it may be of great service
to you in this road you desire to enter if you understand the method of it and approach the service of
Christ accordingly, and as you ought.

Unbounded glory hereafter is promised to
those who faithfully serve God and cleave to God
according to the rule of God's system. But the
severest penalties are in store for those who have
carried it out carelessly and coldly and have failed to
show God fruits of holiness corresponding to what
they professed or what they were believed to be. As
Scripture says, *"It is better that you should not vow than
that you should vow and not fulfill it,"* and *"Accursed is the
one who is slack in doing the work of the Lord."* Therefore
you were for a long while declined by us. It is not

that we did not desire with all our hearts to secure your salvation and the salvation of all or did not care to go out of our way to meet those who are longing to be converted to Christ. But we feared that if we received you rashly we might make ourselves guilty of levity in the sight of God and make you incur a yet heavier punishment, if, when you had been too easily admitted by us without realizing the responsibility of this profession, you had afterwards turned out a deserter or lukewarm. So you should first learn the actual reason for the renunciation of the world. When you have seen this, you can be taught more plainly what you ought to do.

Renunciation is nothing but the evidence of the cross and of mortification. You must know that today you are dead to this world and its deeds and desires. As the apostle says, *"the world has been crucified to me, and I to the world."* Consider therefore the demands of the cross under the sign of which you should live in this life from now on. *It is no longer I who live, but it is Christ who lives in me,* who was crucified for you. We must therefore pass our time in this life in that fashion and form in which he was crucified for us on the cross so that (as David says), *"our flesh trembles for fear of the Lord."* In this way we fulfill the command of the Lord that says, *"Whoever does not take up the cross and follow me is not worthy of me."* But perhaps you will ask how anyone can carry a cross continually? How can anyone who is alive be crucified? Hear briefly how this is.

The fear of the Lord is our cross. As one who is

crucified no longer has the power of moving or turning his limbs in any direction he pleases, so we also ought to fix our wishes and desires—not according to what is pleasant and delightful to us now, but according to the law of the Lord. Those who are fastened to the wood of the cross no longer consider things present, nor think about their likes, nor are perplexed by anxiety and care for the next day, nor disturbed by any desire of possession, nor inflamed by any pride or strife or rivalry. They do not grieve at present injuries or remember past ones. While they still breathe in the body, they consider themselves dead to all earthly things. So we also, when crucified by the fear of the Lord, ought to be dead indeed to all these things—not only to vices of the flesh but also to all earthly things, having the eye of our minds fixed where we hope at each moment that we are soon to pass.

Beware therefore that you never take again any of those things that you renounced and, contrary to the Lord's command, *turn back* from the field of evangelical work *to get a coat* that you had stripped off. Do not sink back to the low and earthly lusts and desires of this world and in defiance of Christ's word come down from the rod of perfection and dare to take up again any of those things that you have renounced and forsaken. Beware that you remember nothing of your family or of your former affections, that you are not called back to the cares and anxieties of this world. As our Lord says, *"No one who puts a hand to the plow and looks back is fit for the kingdom of God."*

Beware in case, when you have begun to dip into the knowledge of the Psalms and of this life, you be little by little puffed up and think of reviving that pride that now at your beginning you have trampled underfoot in the ardor of faith and in fullest humility. Thus (as the apostle says), *"building up again the very things that you once tore down, you demonstrate that you are a transgressor."* Instead, be careful to continue to the end in that state of nakedness in which you made profession in the sight of God and of his angels. In this humility and patience, with which you persevered for ten days before the doors and begged with many tears to be admitted into the monastery, you should not only continue but also increase and go forward. For it is too bad that when you ought to be carried on from the basics and beginnings and go forward to perfection, you should begin to fall back from these to worse things. For not one who begins these things, but *the one who endures to the end will be saved.*

BEGINNING IN PRAYER

From *Conferences*, Conference 9, Chapters 2–4

This selection and the next two are from the conversations with Abba Simon on prayer. Here he talks about how our attitudes and conduct outside our prayer times will affect our ability to pray wholeheartedly.

The aim of every monk and the perfection of his heart tend to continual and unbroken perseverance in prayer. As far as it is allowed to human frailty, he strives to acquire an immovable tranquillity of mind and a perpetual purity, for the sake of which we seek untiringly and constantly to practice all bodily labors as well as contrition of spirit. There is a sort of reciprocal and inseparable union between these two. For just as the crown of the building of all virtues is the perfection of prayer, so unless everything has been united and held together by this as its crown, it cannot possibly remain strong and stable. Lasting and continual calmness in prayer, of which we are speaking, cannot be secured or consummated without them. Neither can those virtues that lay its foundations be fully gained without persistence in it. And so we shall not be able in a brief discourse either to treat the effect of prayer properly or to penetrate to its main end, which is acquired by laboring at all virtues, unless first we enumerate and discuss all those things which for its sake must be either rejected or secured. As the parable in the Gospel teaches, whatever concerns the building of that spiritual and most lofty tower must be reckoned up and carefully considered beforehand. These things, even when prepared, will be of no use nor allow the lofty height of perfection to be properly placed upon them unless we begin with a clearance of all faults. We must also dig up the decayed and dead rubbish of the passions and lay the strong foundations of simplicity and humility on the solid and (so to speak) living soil of our breasts, or rather on that rock of the gospel. By being built in this way this tower of spiritual virtues will rise and be able to stand unmoved and be raised to the utmost heights of heaven in full assurance of its stability. For if it rests on such foundations, then though heavy storms of passions break over it, though mighty torrents of persecutions beat against it like a battering ram, though a furious tempest of spiritual foes dash against it and attack it, yet not only will no ruin overtake it, but the onslaught will not injure it in the slightest degree.

In order that we may offer up prayer with that earnestness and purity with which we ought, we must by all means observe these rules: First, we must entirely get rid of all anxiety about things of the flesh. Next, we must leave no room for the care or even the recollection of any business affairs. Similarly, we must also lay aside all backbiting, empty and incessant chattering, and buffoonery. Above all, anger and disturbing gloominess must be entirely destroyed, and the deadly taint of lust and covetousness be torn out by the roots. When these and similar faults that are also visible to the eyes of others are entirely removed and cut off, and when a purification and cleansing brought about by pure simplicity and innocence have taken place, then first there must be laid the secure foundations of a deep humility which may be able to support a tower that will reach the sky. Next the spiritual structure of the virtues must be built up on them. The soul must be kept free from all conversation and from roving thoughts so that it may little by little begin to rise to the contemplation of God and to spiritual insight. For whatever our minds have been thinking of before the hour of prayer is sure to occur to us while we are praying through the activity of the memory. So whatever we want to find ourselves like while we are praying is what we ought to prepare ourselves to be before the time for prayer. For the mind in prayer is formed by its previous condition. When we are applying ourselves to prayer, the images of the same actions and words and thoughts will dance before our eyes. They will either make us angry or gloomy or recall our former lust and business or make us shake with foolish laughter (which I am ashamed to speak of) at some silly joke or smile at some action or fly back to our previous conversation. Therefore if we do not want anything to haunt us while we are praying, we should be careful before our prayer to exclude it from the shrine of our hearts. Then we may fulfill the apostle's injunctions to *"pray without ceasing"* and *"lift up holy hands without anger or argument."* We shall not be able to carry out that charge unless our minds, purified from all stains of sin and given over to virtue, feed on the continual contemplation of almighty God.

The nature of the soul is aptly compared to a very fine feather or very light wing. If it has not been damaged or spoiled by any moisture falling on it, it is borne aloft almost naturally to the heights of heaven by the lightness of its nature and the aid of the slightest breath. But if it is weighted by any moisture falling upon it and penetrating it, it will not only not be carried away by its natural lightness into any aerial flights but will actually be dragged down to the depths of earth by the weight of the moisture it has received. So also the soul, if it is not weighted with faults that touch it and the cares of this world or damaged by the moisture of injurious lusts, will be raised by the natural blessing of its own purity and borne aloft to the heights by the light breath of spiritual meditation. Leaving things low and earthly, it will be transported to those that are heavenly and invisible. So we are well warned by the Lord's command: *"Be on guard so that your hearts are not weighed down with dissipation and drunkenness and the worries of this life."* If we want our prayers to reach not only the sky but what is beyond the sky, let us be careful to reduce the soul, purged from all earthly faults and purified from every stain, to its natural lightness. Then our prayers may rise to God unchecked by the weight of any sin.

☒ The Lord's Prayer

From *Conferences*, Conference 9, Chapters 18–24

Abba Simon, like many other Christian teachers, finds the height of prayer summarized in the petitions of the Lord's Prayer.

There follows a still more sublime and exalted condition that is brought about by the contemplation of God alone and by fervent love. In this condition the mind, transporting and flinging itself into love for God, addresses God most familiarly as its own Father with a piety of its own. The formula of the Lord's Prayer teaches us that we should earnestly seek this condition, saying, *"Our Father."* When we confess with our own mouths that the God and Lord of the universe is our Father, we claim that we have been called from our condition as slaves to adoption as children. We add next *"in heaven,"* so that, by shunning with the utmost horror all lingering in this present life, which we pass upon this earth as a pilgrimage, and anything else that separates us by a great distance from our Father, we may instead hurry with all eagerness to that country where we confess that our Father dwells. May we not allow anything of this kind, which would make us unworthy of our profession and the dignity of an adoption of this kind, to deprive us as a disgrace to our Father's inheritance and so make us incur the wrath of God's justice and severity. When we have advanced to this state and condition of adoption, we will be inflamed with the piety that belongs to good children. Then we will devote all our energies to promoting not our own profit but our Father's glory, saying to God, *"Hallowed be your name."* When we testify that our desire and our joy are God's glory, we become imitators of Christ, who said, *"Those who speak on their own seek their own glory; but the one who seeks the glory of him who sent him is true, and there is nothing false in him."* And so when we say to God, *"Hallowed be your name,"* we say in other words, "Make us, O Father, such that we may be able both to understand and to take in what it means to hallow you, or at any rate that you may be seen to be hallowed in our spiritual conduct." This is fulfilled in our case when people see our *good works and give glory to our Father in heaven.*

The second petition of the pure heart desires that the kingdom of its Father may come at once. This refers first of all to its coming where Christ reigns day by day in the saints (when the devil's rule is cast out and God begins to hold sway over us and love reigns in our hearts together with tranquillity and humility). It also refers to what is promised in due time to all God's children. Then Christ will say to them, *"Come, you that are blessed by my Father, inherit the kingdom prepared for you from the foundation of the world."*

The third petition is *"Your will be done, on earth as it is in heaven."* There can now be no grander prayer than to wish that earthly things may be made equal with heavenly things. What else is it to say, *"Your will be done, on earth as it is in heaven"* than to ask that people may be like angels and that as God's will is always fulfilled by them in heaven, so also all those who are on earth may do not their own but God's will? Again, no one could say this from the heart except one who believed that God disposes for our good all visible things, whether fortunate or unfortunate, and that God is more careful in providing for our good and salvation than we ourselves are for ourselves.

Next: *"Give us this day our daily bread."* Where it says "daily" it shows that without it we cannot live a spiritual life for a single day. Where it says "this day" it shows that it must be received daily and that yesterday's supply of it is not enough. It must be given to us today also in the same manner. And our daily need of it suggests to us that we ought at all times to offer up this prayer, because there is no day on which we have no need to strengthen the heart of our inner person by eating and receiving it.

"And forgive us our debts, as we also have forgiven our debtors." Unspeakable mercy of God! It has given us a form of prayer and taught us a system of life acceptable to God, and by the requirements of the form given, in which Christ charged us always to pray, it has torn up the roots of both anger and sorrow. And it also gives to those who pray an opportunity and reveals to them a way by which they may move a merciful and kindly judgment of God to be pronounced over them. Somehow it gives us a power by which we can moderate the sentence of our

Judge, drawing God to forgive our offenses by the example of our forgiveness, when we say to God, "Forgive us as we also forgive." And so without anxiety and in confidence from this prayer we may ask for pardon of our own offenses if we have been forgiving toward our own debtors and not just toward those of our Lord. For some of us, which is very bad, are inclined to show ourselves calm and most merciful in regard to those things that are done to God's detriment, however great the crimes may be. But we are found to be most hard and unyielding in demanding repayment of debts to ourselves, even in the case of the most trifling wrongs. Those then who do not forgive others who have offended them from their hearts call down on themselves not forgiveness but condemnation by this prayer. By their own profession they ask that they themselves may be judged more severely, saying, "Forgive me as I also have forgiven." So if we want to be judged mercifully, we ought also to be merciful toward those who have sinned against us.

Next there follows: *"And do not bring us to the time of trial,"* on which there arises no unimportant question, for if we pray that we may not be allowed to be tested, how then will our power of endurance be proved? The clause then, *"do not bring us to the time of trial,"* does not mean do not permit us ever to be tempted, but do not permit us when we fall into temptation to be overcome. Next there follows: *"But rescue us from the evil one,"* that is, do not allow us to be tested by the devil beyond our ability, but *with the testing*

God will also provide the way out so that you may be able to endure it.

You see then what the method and form of prayer is that has been proposed to us by the Judge, who is to be prayed to by it. It is a form that contains no petition for riches, no thought of honors, no request for power and might, no mention of bodily health and of temporal life. For God, the Author of Eternity, would have us ask for nothing uncertain, nothing paltry, and nothing temporal.

So, then, this prayer seems to contain all the fullness of perfection since it was given and commanded by the Lord's own authority. But it lifts those to whom it belongs to that much higher condition of which we spoke above, that standing in fire which is known and experienced by very few and is, to tell the truth, indescribable. It transcends all human thoughts and is not distinguished by any sound of the voice or movement of the tongue or pronounced words. Instead, the mind, enlightened by heavenly light flowing in, pours forth richly as from a copious fountain a burst of thoughts. In the shortest possible space of time it expresses such great things that the mind cannot talk about them or even recall them when it returns to its usual condition.

PRAYER WITHOUT CEASING

From *Conferences*, Conference 10, Chapter 10

As one method of praying without ceasing, Abba Simon offers a brief formula for prayer on any occasion or in any condition. It is the first verse of the seventieth Psalm.

For keeping up continual recollection of God this pious formula is to be ever set before you: *"Be pleased, O God, to deliver me. O Lord, make haste to help me!"* This verse has not unreasonably been picked out from the whole of Scripture for this purpose. It embraces all the feelings that can be implanted in human nature and can be satisfactorily adapted to every condition and all assaults. It contains an invocation of God against every danger. It contains humble and pious confession. It contains the watchfulness of anxiety and continual fear. It contains the thought of one's own weakness, confidence in the answer, and the assurance of a present and ever ready help. It contains the glow of love. This verse is an impregnable wall for all who are laboring under the attacks of demons, as well as an impenetrable coat of mail and a strong shield. It warns those of us whose lot is spiritual success and delight of heart that we ought not to be at all elated or puffed up by our happy condition. It reminds us that this condition cannot last without God as our protector while it implores God not only always but even speedily to help us.

I am affected by the passion of gluttony. I ask for food of which the desert knows nothing, and in the squalid desert there are wafted to me odors of royal dainties. I find that even against my will I am drawn to long for them. I must at once say, *"Be pleased, O God, to deliver me. O Lord, make haste to help me!"* I am incited to anticipate the hour fixed for supper, or I am trying with great sorrow of heart to keep to the limits of the right and regular simple fare. I must cry out with groans, *"Be pleased, O God, to deliver me. O Lord, make haste to help me!"* When I come to supper, at the bidding of the proper hour I loathe taking food and am prevented from eating anything to satisfy the requirements of nature. I must cry with a sigh, *"Be pleased, O God, to deliver me. O Lord, make haste to help me!"*

When I want for the sake of steadfastness of heart to apply myself to reading, a headache interferes and stops me. At the third hour sleep glues my head to the sacred page, and I am forced either to overstep or to anticipate the time assigned to rest. In the same way I must cry out, *"Be pleased, O God, to deliver me. O Lord, make haste to help me!"* Sleep is withdrawn from my eyes, and for many nights I find myself worn out with sleeplessness caused by the devil. All repose and rest by night is kept away from my eyelids. I must sigh and pray, *"Be pleased, O God, to deliver me. O Lord, make haste to help me!"*

I am disturbed by the pangs of anger, covetousness, and gloominess, and driven to disturb the peaceful state in which I was, and which was dear to me.

In order that I may not be carried away by raging passion into bitterness, I must cry out with deep groans, *"Be pleased, O God, to deliver me. O Lord, make haste to help me!"* I am tried by being puffed up by weariness of heart, vanity, and pride. My mind flatters itself somewhat with subtle thoughts concerning the coldness and carelessness of others. That this dangerous suggestion of the enemy may not get the mastery over me, I must pray with all contrition of heart, *"Be pleased, O God, to deliver me. O Lord, make haste to help me!"* I have gained the grace of humility and simplicity, and by continually mortifying my spirit have got rid of the swellings of pride. So that the *foot of arrogance* may not again *tread on me* and *the hand of the wicked drive me away* and that I may not be more seriously damaged by elation at my success, I must cry with all my might, *"Be pleased, O God, to deliver me. O Lord, make haste to help me!"*

I am on fire with innumerable and various wanderings of soul and shiftiness of heart and cannot collect my scattered thoughts. I cannot even pour forth my prayer without interruption from useless images and memories of conversations and actions. I feel myself tied down by such dryness and barrenness that I feel I cannot give birth to any spiritual ideas. In order that I may be set free from this wretched state of mind, from which I cannot escape by any number of sighs and groans, I must surely cry out, *"Be pleased, O God, to deliver me. O Lord, make haste to help me!"* Again, I feel that by the visitation of the Holy Spirit I have gained purpose of soul, steadfastness of thought, keenness of heart, together with an ineffable joy and transport of mind. In the exuberance of spiritual feelings I have perceived by a sudden illumination from the Lord an abounding revelation of most holy ideas that were formerly altogether hidden from me. In order that I may be allowed to linger for a longer time in them I must often and anxiously exclaim, *"Be pleased, O God, to deliver me. O Lord, make haste to help me!"*

Encompassed by nightly horrors of devils, I am agitated and disturbed by the appearances of unclean spirits. My very hope of life and salvation is withdrawn by the horror of fear. Flying to the safe refuge of this verse, I will cry out with all my might, *"Be pleased, O God, to deliver me. O Lord, make haste to help me!"* When I have been restored by the Lord's consolation and cheered by his coming, I feel as if I am surrounded by countless thousands of angels. That the strength of this courage may, by God's grace, remain in me still longer, I must cry out with all my powers, *"Be pleased, O God, to deliver me. O Lord, make haste to help me!"*

We must then ceaselessly and continuously pour forth the prayer of this verse, in adversity that we may be delivered, in prosperity that we may be preserved and not puffed up. Whatever work you are doing, or office you are holding, or journey you are making, do not cease to chant this. When you are going to bed or eating or in the last necessities of nature, think on this. Let sleep come upon you still considering this verse, till having been molded by the constant use of it, you grow accustomed to repeat it even in your sleep. When you wake let it be the first thing to come into your mind. When you rise from your bed let it send you down on your knees and then forth to all your work and business. Let it follow you about all day long.

KEEPING THE MIND ON GOD

From *Conferences*, Conference 1, Chapters 15–18

No matter how deep our prayers may be, we still have to deal with distracting thoughts. Here, Abba Moses offers his advice for minimizing such distractions.

The contemplation of God is gained in a variety of ways. For we not only discover God by admiring God's incomprehensible essence, a thing that still lies hidden in the hope of the promise, but we see God through the greatness of creation, the consideration of God's justice, and the aid of God's daily providence. With pure minds we contemplate what God has done with God's saints in every generation. With trembling hearts we admire the power with which God governs, directs, and rules all things; we admire the vastness of God's knowledge and that eye of God's from which no secrets of the heart can lie hidden. We gaze in unbounded admiration on God's mercy, which with unwearied patience endures the countless sins that are every moment being committed under God's very eyes. But there are numberless other considerations of this sort that arise in our minds according to the character of our lives and the purity of our hearts. Through such considerations, God is either seen by pure eyes or embraced.

GERMANUS: How is it then, that even against our will and without our knowledge idle thoughts steal upon us so subtly and secretly that it is fearfully hard not merely to drive them away, but even to grasp and seize them? Can a mind sometimes be found free from them and never attacked by illusions of this kind?

MOSES: It is impossible for the mind not to be approached by thoughts, but it is in the power of every earnest person either to admit them or to reject them. As then their rising up does not entirely depend on ourselves, so the rejection or admission of them lies in our own power. But because we said that it is impossible for the mind not to be approached by thoughts, you must not lay everything to the charge of the assault or to those spirits who strive to instill them into us. Otherwise, there would not remain any free will in us, nor would efforts for our improvement be in our power. But it is, I say, to a great extent in our power to improve the character of our thoughts and to let either holy and spiritual thoughts or earthly ones grow up in our hearts. For this purpose we employ frequent reading and continual meditation on the Scriptures to give us an opportunity for spiritual recollection. For this purpose we use the frequent singing of Psalms to provide constant feelings of compunction. We also use earnest vigils and fasts and prayers, that the mind may be brought low and not mind earthly things but contemplate things celestial. If these things are dropped and carelessness creeps on us, the mind, hardened with the foulness of sin, is sure to incline in a worldly direction and fall away.

This movement of the heart is not unsuitably illustrated by the comparison of a mill wheel, which the headlong rush of water whirls round with revolving impetus. It can never stop its work so long as it is driven round by the action of the water. But it is in the power of the man who directs it to decide whether he will have wheat or barley or darnel ground by it. Whatever the man in charge of the business puts into it certainly must be crushed by it. So then the mind also through the trials of the present life is driven about by the torrents of temptations pouring in upon it from all sides and cannot be free from the flow of thoughts. But it will provide the character of the thoughts that it should either throw off or admit for itself by the efforts of its own earnestness and diligence. If, as we said, we constantly return to meditation on the Holy Scriptures and raise our memory toward the recollection of spiritual things and the desire of perfection and the hope of future bliss, spiritual thoughts are sure to rise from this and cause the mind to dwell on those things on which we have been meditating. But if we are overcome by sloth or carelessness and spend our time in idle gossip or are entangled in the cares of this world and unnecessary anxieties, the result will be that a sort of species of tares will spring up and afford an injurious occupation for our hearts, and as our Lord and Savior says, *"where the treasure"* of your works or purpose *"is, there your heart"* is sure to *"be also."*

# PERFECTION IN LOVE

From *Conferences*, Conference 11, Chapters 8–9

This final selection is taken from the conference with Abba Chaeremon and deals with Christian perfection, the life lived out of love for God.

There is a great difference between those who put out the fire of sin within themselves by fear of hell or hope of future reward and those who from the feeling of divine love have a horror of sin itself and of uncleanness and keep hold of the virtue of purity simply from the love and longing for purity. They look for no reward from a promise for the future, but delighted with the knowledge of good things present, do everything not from regard to punishment but from delight in virtue. For this condition can neither abuse an opportunity to sin when all human witnesses are absent nor be corrupted by the secret allurements of thoughts. Keeping in its very marrow the love of virtue itself, it not only does not admit into the heart anything that is opposed to it, but actually hates it with the utmost horror. For it is one thing for someone in delight at some present good to hate the stains of sins and of the flesh and another thing to check unlawful desires by contemplating the future reward. And it is one thing to fear present loss and another to dread future punishment. Finally, it is a much greater thing to be unwilling to forsake good

for good's own sake than it is to withhold consent
from evil for fear of evil. For in the former case the
good is voluntary, but in the latter it is constrained
either by fear of punishment or by greed of reward
and more or less violently forced out of a reluctant
party. Those who abstain from the allurements of sin
owing to fear will, whenever the obstacle of fear is
removed, once more return to what they love and so
will not gain any permanent stability in good. Nor
will they ever rest free from attacks, because they will
not secure the sure and lasting peace of chastity. For
where there is the disturbance of warfare there cannot help being the danger of wounds. Those who are
in the midst of the conflict, even though they are
warriors and by fighting bravely inflict frequent and
deadly wounds on their foes, must still sometimes be
pierced by the point of the enemy's sword. But those
who have defeated the attack of sins and now enjoy
the security of peace and have passed on to the love
of virtue itself, will keep this condition of good continually. They are entirely wrapped up in it, because
they believe that nothing can be worse than the loss
of their inmost chastity. For they deem nothing
dearer or more precious than present purity. To
them, a dangerous departure from virtue or a poisonous stain of sin is itself a grievous punishment. To
such, I say, neither will regard for the presence of
another add anything to their goodness nor will solitude take anything away from it. Always and every-
where they bear about with them their conscience as
a judge not only of their actions but also of their

thoughts. So they will especially try to please it, since they know that it cannot be cheated nor deceived, and that they cannot escape it.

If any who rely on the help of God and not on their own efforts have been allowed to acquire this state, they will begin to pass on from the condition of a fearful servant and from a mercenary greed of hope, which seeks not so much the good of the donor as the recompense of reward, to adoption as God's children, where there is no longer fear or greed. That love that never fails stays with them continually. Those who by this love have attained the image and likeness of God will now delight in goodness for the pleasure of goodness itself. Having somehow a like feeling of patience and gentleness, they will no longer be angered by faults of sinners. In compassion and sympathy they will ask for pardon for the infirmities of others. Remembering that for so long they themselves were tested by the stings of similar passions till by the Lord's mercy they were saved, they will feel that, since they are saved from such attacks not by their own exertions but by God's protection, they ought to show not anger but pity to those who go astray. With full peace of mind they will sing to God the following verse: *"You have loosed my bonds. I will offer to you a thanksgiving sacrifice."* Also: *"If the Lord had not been my help, my soul would soon have lived in the land of silence."* And while they continue in this humility of mind, they will be able even to fulfill this Gospel command of perfection: *"Love your enemies, do good to those who hate you, and pray for those who persecute you, so that you may be children of your Father in heaven; for he makes his sun rise on the evil and on the good, and sends rain on the righteous and on the unrighteous."* The blessed John knew that he had attained this feeling when he said, *"We may have boldness on the day of judgment, because as he is, so are we in this world."* For in what can a weak and fragile human nature be like God, except in always showing a calm love in its heart toward the good and the evil, the just and the unjust, in imitation of God, and by doing good for the love of goodness itself? *Those who have been born of God do not sin, because God's seed abides in them; they cannot sin, because they have been born of God.* This must be understood not of all kinds of sins, but only of mortal sins. For it is an impossibility for any one of the saints not to fall into those trivial faults that are committed by word, thought, ignorance, forgetfulness, necessity, will, and surprise. Though quite different from that sin that is said to be mortal, they still cannot be free from fault and blame.

Appendix

Reading Spiritual Classics for Personal and Group Formation

Many Christians today are searching for more spiritual depth, for something more than simply being good church members. That quest may send them to the spiritual practices of New Age movements or of Eastern religions such as Zen Buddhism. Christians, though, have their own long spiritual tradition, a tradition rich with wisdom, variety, and depth.

The great spiritual classics testify to that depth. They do not concern themselves with mystical flights for a spiritual elite. Rather, they contain very practical advice and insights that can support and shape the spiritual growth of any Christian. We can all benefit by sitting at the feet of the masters (both male and female) of Christian spirituality.

Reading spiritual classics is different from most of the reading we do. We have learned to read to master a text and extract information from it. We tend to read quickly, to get through a text. And we summarize as we read, seeking the main point. In reading spiritual classics, though, we allow the text to master and form us. Such formative reading goes more slowly, more reflectively, allowing time for God to speak to us through the text. God's word for us may come as easily from a minor point or even an aside as from the major point.

Formative reading requires that you approach the text in humility. Read as a seeker, not as an expert. Don't demand that the text meet your expectations for what an "enlightened" author should write. Humility means accepting the author as another imperfect human, a product of his or her own time and situation. Learn to celebrate what is foundational in an author's writing without being overly disturbed by what is peculiar to the author's life and times. Trust the text as a gift from both God and the author, offered to you for your benefit—to help you grow in Christ.

To read formatively, you must also slow down. Feel free to reread a passage that seems to speak specially to you. Stop from time to time to reflect on what you have been reading. Keep a journal for these reflections. Often the act of writing can itself prompt further, deeper reflection. Keep your notebook open and your pencil in hand as you read. You might not get back to that wonderful insight later. Don't worry that you are not getting through an entire passage— or even the first paragraph! Formative reading is about depth rather than breadth, quality rather than quantity. As you read, seek God's direction for your own life. Timeless truths have their place but may not be what is most important for your own formation here and now.

As you read the passage, you might keep some of these questions running through your mind:

• How is what I'm reading true of my own life? Where does it reflect my own *experience*?

- How does this text challenge me? What new *direction* does it offer me?
- What must I change to put what I am reading into practice? How can I *incarnate* it, let this word become flesh in my life?

You might also devote special attention to sections that upset you. What is the source of the disturbance? Do you want to argue theology? Are you turned off by cultural differences? Or have you been skewered by an insight that would turn your life upside down if you took it seriously? Let your journal be a dialogue with the text.

If you find yourself moving from reading the text to chewing over its implications to praying, that's great! Spiritual reading is really the first step in an ancient way of prayer called *lectio divina* or "divine reading." Reading leads naturally into reflection on what you have read (meditation). As you reflect on what the text might mean for your life, you may well want to ask for God's help in living out any new insights or direction you have perceived (prayer). Sometimes such prayer may lead you further into silently abiding in God's presence (contemplation). And, of course, the process is only really completed when it begins to make a difference in the way we live (incarnation).

As good as it is to read spiritual classics in solitude, it is even better to join with others in a small group for mutual formation or "spiritual direction in common." This is *not* the same as a study group that talks *about* spiritual classics. A group for mutual formation would have similar goals as for an individual's reading: to allow the text to shine its light on the *experiences* of the group members, to suggest new *directions* for their lives and practical ways of *incarnating* these directions. Such a group might agree to focus on one short passage from a classic at each meeting (even if members have read more). Discussion usually goes much deeper if all the members have already read and reflected on the passage before the meeting and bring their journals.

Such groups need to watch for several potential problems. It is easy to go off on a tangent (especially if it takes the focus off the members' own experience and onto generalities). At such times a group leader might bring the group's attention back to the text: "What does our author say about that?" Or, "How do we experience that in our own lives?" When a group member shares a problem, others may be tempted to try to "fix" it. This is much less helpful than sharing similar experiences and how they were handled (for good or ill). "Sharing" someone else's problems (whether that person is in or out of the group) should be strongly discouraged.

One person could be designated as leader, to be responsible for opening and closing prayers; to be the first to share or respond to the text; and to keep notes during the discussion to highlight recurring themes, challenges, directives, or practical steps. These responsibilities could also be shared among several members of the group or rotated.

For further information about formative reading of spiritual classics, try *A Practical Guide to Spiritual Reading* by Susan Annette Muto. *Shaped by the Word* by Robert Mulholland (Upper Room Books) covers formative reading of the Bible. *Good Things Happen: Experiencing Community in Small Groups* by Dick Westley is an excellent resource on forming small groups of all kinds.